Lost Buildings
Peak District

Lindsey Porter

Lost Buildings of the Peak District

Lindsey Porter

Landmark Publishing

Published by

LANDMARK
Publishing Ltd ● ● ● ●

Ashbourne Hall, Cokayne Ave
Ashbourne, Derbyshire DE6 1EJ England
Tel: (01335) 347349 Fax: (01335) 347303
e-mail: landmark@clara.net
web site: www.landmarkpublishing.co.uk

ISBN 13: 978-1-84306-358-2

© Lindsey Porter 2007

British Library Cataloguing in Publication Data: a catalogue
record for this book is available from the British Library.

Printed by Gutenberg Press, Malta

Designed by Michelle Hunt

Front Cover: Throwley Hall, Ilam

Back Cover Top: Derwent Hall, Derwent

Back cover bottom left: Royal Hotel, Matlock Bath

Back cover bottom right: Parwich Youth Hostel

Page 3: Dain's Mill, Upper Hulme

Contents

Introduction

Maxwell Craven and Michael Stanley's book *Lost Houses of Derbyshire* highlighted the number of country houses that we have lost over the years and their list ignored urban and rural villas, town houses of the aristocracy etc. Over the border into Staffordshire, *Lost Houses of North Staffordshire* by Cath Walton and myself, took a look at what this much smaller area had lost. Indeed the Dove Valley area alone has lost at least a dozen north of Uttoxeter, with another dozen around Leek and Cheadle.

It set my mind thinking about what other buildings had gone and my thoughts polarised on the Peak. This is not a book about architectural gems; I have tried to portray examples of different types of useage and indeed, I have included a few properties that have survived but where the type of user has changed.

There is definitely room for another book on a group of substantial buildings of which only a few examples are included here – hotels. The area has lost some rather large and opulent examples – The Royal at Matlock Bath and The Empire at Buxton for instance. They were massive buildings built in a different age, which never recovered after The Great War.

Focusing on what has now gone gives us an opportunity to reflect on what we have now and how quickly old familiar properties are quickly swept away. Assembling the images for this book made me realise how substantial have been the changes in Ashbourne. Sometimes change is clearly for the better, but did we really have to let the Bath House in Park Road go? Was the demolition of the H-Block factory building at Coopers Textiles in the town's best interests? I am sure similar comments could be, and probably are, being aired elsewhere too. The future if the former Haddon Hydro Hotel in Buxton (see p.86) springs to mind.

I hope this book allows you to reflect on what we have lost and that you find it of interest as a result. I could not see much advantage to providing a map of locations, but have given a brief location in many of the captions.

Acknowledgements:

I wish to thank the following for their assistance in the compilation of these photographs and hope I have not excluded anyone.

James Allsopp; David Alsop; M. Burton; Buxton Library; Derbyshire Library Services, Matlock and Belper; Ron Duggins; The Duke of Devonshire & The Trustees of the Chatsworth Settlement; Tim Eades; Yvonne Goldstraw; Sheila Hine; Charles Hurt; Robin Hurt; David McPhie; Dianne Naylor; Pam Paget-Tomlinson; Harry Parker; Dr. J.H., (Jim) Rieuwerts; Sentinel Newspapers Ltd., Ian & Grace Shaw; Mike Smith; Charles Stanton; William Salt Library, Stafford; Vega Wilkinson; Peter Wilson.

Bibliographical Sources are:

Combes, I.A.H., *Anglican Churches of Derbyshire*, 2004

Craven, M., & Stanley, M., *The Derbyshire Country House*, Vols 1 & 2, 2001

Harris, H., *Industrial Archaeology of the Peak District*, 1971

Hine, S., *Around Meerbrook*, 2004

Langham, M., *Buxton A People's History*, 2001

Naylor, D., *The Chatsworth Villages: Beeley, Edensor & Pilsley*, 2005

Nixon, F., *Industrial Archaeology of Derbyshire*, 1969

Parker, H.M., & Willies, L., *Peakland Lead Mines & Miners*, 1979

Pevsner, N., *The Buildings of England, Derbyshire*

Pilkington, J., *A View of the Present State of Derbyshire*, 1789

Porter, L., *Victorian Ashbourne*, 2000

Porter, L., *Spirit of Ashbourne Vol 2*, 2000

Rieuwerts, J.H., *Derbyshire's Old Lead Mines & Miners*, 1972

Smith, M., *Spirit of the High Peak*, 2000

Walton, C., & Porter, L., *Lost Houses of North Staffordshire*, 2006

Derwent Hall, Derwent

Built in 1672 on the bank of the River Derwent, this house passed through various families until being sold to the Duke of Norfolk in 1886. He added a southeast wing and used the estate for shooting parties, no doubt associating with the 8th Duke of Devonshire's social parties at that time. The construction of Ladybower Reservoir saw the demise of the whole village, the hall, being used as a youth hostel in the 1930s. It was opened in 1932 by the Prince of Wales. In the curtain wall was a gate with a carving of 'Peeping Tom' looking over the wall to the river. He now resides at Castleton Youth Hostel being given to the YHA by the Water Board.

The north west corner, with peeping Tom (see overleaf).

Above: Peeping Tom.

Below: The west front.

Drawing Room, Derwent Hall.

The drawing room (above) and entrance hall (below).

Fire Place Entrance Hall, Derwent Hall.

The garden pond and chapel, south front.

West front and drive. The river is to the left and Peeping Tom by the second set of gate posts.

Osmaston Manor, Osmaston, Nr Ashbourne

Built in 1846-9 for Francis Wright. His descendant, Sir Peter Walker inherited the Okeover Hall estate c.1955. A condition was that he took the name Okeover and lived there. No use could be found for the manor and it was demolished in 1965. The architect was Henry Stevens, who also built the church – aligned with the manor drive – in 1845. It was one of the earliest Gothic Revival churches in Derbyshire and perhaps one of the best.

The east front.

The north front.

Two views of the conservatory on the south side of the house.

Barbrook, Edensor

This was Joseph Paxton's house, home and office. The core was an 18th-century cottage, enlarged from time to time. It had a conservatory, in keeping with Victorian fashion, plus a lily house. Here the Amazonian water lily (Victoria Regia) flowered in this country for the first time in 1849, ahead of the plants at Kew. The Dowager Duchess, in her book *The Estate* states that the Duke's agent lived here until he died in 1946, the house being left empty after that. It deteriorated and was demolished in 1963. The lodge survives, with a copper roof, distinctive eaves board and canopy supported by cast iron columns.

Ashbourne Hall, Ashbourne

A pleasant house at the end of Ashbourne's main street, the stairwell may be Jacobean (pers.com., Maxwell Craven) and the adjacent rooms may well be from a later house known to Bonnie Prince Charlie, who slept here in 1745. The house extended further east than now on its south front. Altered extensively again, it ended up with a west wing looking more like a factory than a gentleman's residence. It became a hotel in 1900, but the house and its 200-acre park was later sub-divided and the house sold in small portions. A rump survives, with its park now playing fields, a memorial ground and a housing estate.

Errwood Hall, Goyt Valley

The house was built in the first half of the 1840s by Samuel Grimshawe and was situated on the west side of the valley, above the ancient packhorse bridge (Goyt Bridge). It was Italianate in style with spectacular gardens planted with rhododendrons, some of which survive. The house passed to the maternal line and into the Gosselin family of Bengeo Hall in Herefordshire. Taking the name of Grimshawe, they lived here until 1930 when the estate was purchased by Stockport Corporation. With the construction of Ferneylee Reservoir, the house was demolished, just part of the external wall of the south-front remaining. Part of the chapel plasterwork apparently survives in the Stockport Council Offices. In the early 1960s, Errwood Reservoir was constructed, submerging more of the former estate. Bottom photo: remains in the early 1960s.

Snelston Hall, Snelston

Influenced by the massive building work at Alton Towers and perhaps that at Ilam also, John Harrison instructed Lewis Cottingham to design a new house at Snelston. After several designs, work started in 1827 on a Gothic Revival building. This survived the loss of many local houses, including Ilam (also Gothic Revival style) in the 1930s but was to become impractical as a home and was demolished in 1953. The Stanton family moved into the refurbished former stable block and still reside there. The hall had many features similar to Alton, including a Great Hall, well lit by a massive window.

Above: The south front.

Left: The west front.

Opposite : Two views of the interior.

Okeover Hall, Okeover

This house, built within a protective moat, was drawn to illustrate Plot's *History of Staffordshire*, of 1686. It was replaced by a Georgian house, adjacent to the church, now the east wing of the current house. A short south wing was extended in the 1960s. Shown here are the 17th century house and the truncated south wing prior to extension.

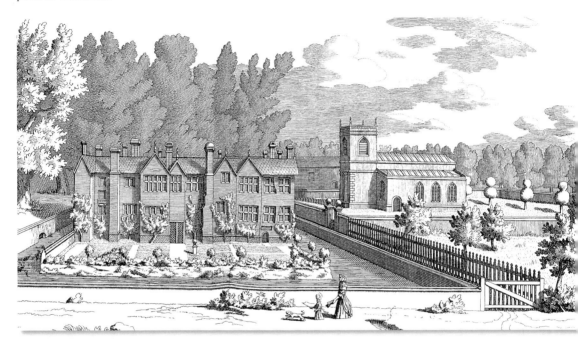

Ilam Hall, Ilam

Built by Jesse Watts Russell, work commenced in 1821. It replaced an earlier house, the home of the Port family. Built of local gritstone from Stanton (to the southwest) it had a peach-coloured appearance when built. Jesse Watts Russell was an enthusiast of the Gothic Revival style of architecture and this house was an early example. It was sold to Mr. Hanbury in 1875. He became President of the Board of Agriculture but died in 1903. Lying empty in the 1930s, it was offered to the National Trust, who initially declined it. Much of the estate in Dovedale was, however, gifted to the Trust. The YHA took the building on, but the formal rooms were demolished, leaving the entrance hall and service wings. These exist to this day, in the ownership of the National Trust.

Below: The house of the Port family.

The north front.

A drawing in the Hurt family archives of Ilam.

The east, or garden, front.

Swainsley Hall, near Butterton

Built in 1868 by Richard Roscoe, a London solicitor. The original house was extended at both ends, the western extension being rebuilt after a fire in the early 1950s. Here the original building is seen with the western extension. Roscoe's wife Honora was the granddaughter of John Taylor, the celebrated mineral agent who worked for the 6th Duke of Devonshire in the first half of the 19th century. She came to Ecton as a child with John Taylor and presumably the decision to build Swainsley here was her wish.

Swythamley Hall, Heaton

This early 19th-Century house is shown here in 1831 (from a sale notice). It was subsequently extended twice and is now apartments.

Alton Castle, Alton

This Norman castle was built in c.1175 by Bertram de Verdun who founded nearby Croxden Abbey. After the Civil War, it fell into disrepair, as shown in a drawing by Buck of 1731 and was rebuilt by the 16th Earl of Shrewsbury in 1847. Part of the west front remains (compare the left hand side below with p32).

The castle from the river.

The surviving part of the west wall of the castle.

Another view of the west wall of the castle.

Bretton Clough Farm

This was formerly situated in Bretton Clough, north of Bretton. Once two farms, the left hand one was Hawley's Farm and the right hand one was Fairest Clough Farm, dating from 1782. It was demolished in 1935. The last occupant was Joseph Townsend, who rented the farm. His thoughts on his rent were preserved in a wonderful quote: "two houses and over 100 ackers o'land for forty pun a year rent an it were as dear as hellfire at that". Hill farms have now found new uses as second homes and holiday accommodation. Bretton Clough would have attracted a useful premium today!

White Cliffe Farm, Parwich

This small farmhouse survives, but is not included here for its house. In the foreground is the house mere. It was originally used for home and shippon until mains water arrived. Like many others, this one was filled in although only in recent times – 2001. This was probably deeper than most. They were expensive to construct. One at the Newhaven House Hotel cost over £26.00 in 1792, perhaps the best part of £5,000.00 now; albeit a larger one, which still survives east of the A515.

Doublers Row, River Dane, Gradbach

These ruins of a row of terraced cottages situated adjacent to the River Dane are to be found upstream of the Gradbach Youth Hostel, formerly a silk and later a flax (linen) mill. Believed to have been built as workers cottages for the mill they have deteriorated badly in the last 50 years. Built on the road to the mill, the building below was a stable and also traditionally held to be a lodging house for workers.

Birchinlee

Two views of the temporary village which housed workers building Howden and Derwent dams in the Upper Derwent Valley. Over 50 buildings were erected here.

TOWN HALL & MARKET SQUARE,
DERWENT VALLEY WATER WORKS.

Chatsworth Mill

This mill was built in 1761-2 and the architect was James Paine. It was the estate's flour-mill, grinding cereals, although it ended its working life as an animal feed store. During the 1962 gale that swept across the Peak, two beech trees fell across the building, damaging it beyond repair. Its ruins still remain and the former mill weir on the River Derwent is a popular play area on warm, sunny days in summer.

Carter's Mill, Lathkilldale

An old mine plan dated 1826 shows an 'old watercourse' which commenced close to 'the New Mill', now known as Carter's Mill. The wheel was removed for scrap during World War II. Now only the foundations and two mill stones survive, which may indicate that it only had one pair of stones. The weir survives, impounding a large sheet of water. This water also provided a supply to Mandale Mine, which crossed the river by an aqueduct. (see p.67).

Dain's Mill, Upper Hulme

A corn mill producing oat meal and bran. It was last used in c. 1940 when the dam burst. Most village mills ground oats, the main cereal crop of upland areas.

Cressbrook Mill, Cressbrook

Once Sir Richard Arkwright established his business at Cromford, he rapidly built other cotton mills including Cressbrook in 1779. The later main Georgian block of 1815 survives, but the much later north-light roofed extension on the downstream side and the chimney have gone, with conversion of the site to residential use.

Hartington Cotton Mill

This mill was opened by Thomas Cantrell and existed in the Market Place. Opposite the mill were four cottages, which still survive, with a date-stone bearing the date 1776 and T & JC (Thomas & Jane Cantrell). Pilkington describes the mill as producing cotton, thread, linen and check, employing about 60 people. It burnt down in 1786. The building later became a penny lodging house before being demolished to make way for two houses. It is the two-storey building on the right of the photograph of a group of volunteer soldiers.

Stay Works, Ashbourne

Richard Cooper & Co commenced business in Ashbourne in 1855 moving to premises in Compton in 1860. This building (the Stay Works) was erected in 1870. It was demolished in 1995 and the site is the goods entrance to Sainsburys. The Company enjoyed earlier success, employing 500 people by 1900. The H-block was built in 1912. Coopers were the first corset manufacturer to have an assembly line for corset making. Most of the properties on the two aerial photographs have now gone, including the factory, chapel, railway station and many others.

Froghall Mill

Above: This water mill may initially have been a corn mill, but in the 19th century ground local iron-ore as a colour mill. The ore was bright red and canal boats took vast quantities to the foundries of the Black Country. Ground to a fine dust, the ore was mixed with lime wash to turn it red. The last local mine closed in 1921. The site is now a car-breakers yard, with one building surviving.

Opposite Top: Woodeaves Mill, Fenny Bentley

Built in 1784 as a cotton mill powered by water. The leat was also used as a canal, bringing limestone (to possibly build the mill). It initially was operated by John Cooper who also had a cotton-works at Ashbourne. It was powered by a 250hp engine, supplemented by a 100hp turbine, which had replaced the waterwheel. Put up for sale in 1910 it was then used as a cheese factory before being demolished. The turbine may have dated from 1881, when floods caused a lot of damage to the top weir.

Opposite Bottom: Torr Mill, New Mills

Overshadowed by the Union Road viaduct was this water powered mill, now demolished. So many early Peak District mills could not complete with the Lancashire cotton industry and while some found other uses, many have gone.

Bottom's Mill, Longdendale

One of many properties lost when the Longdendale reservoirs were built by Manchester Corporation between 1866 - 81.

Ecton Copper Mine Engine House, near Warslow

This building housed the first Boulton & Watt winding engine erected in the Midlands. It is on the mine with (probably) the first shaft in the country to pass 1,000ft (303m) deep and the richest in the country in the 1780s. The shaft here is over 1,200ft (364m) deep, the mine itself being 400ft (121m) deeper. The building was erected in 1788. No contemporary illustration survives of it complete with its machinery or chimney, only a series of drawings of the proposed engine and house. The roof was lowered because of wind damage in the 1920s-30s.

New Engine Mine Chimney, Eyam Edge

This chimney was also demolished, in the 1970s, the adjacent shaft being 1,093ft (331m) deep, the deepest on a Derbyshire lead mine. The engine was erected in 1863 and the mine closed in 1884. The beam of the former beam engine is believed to be lodged in the shaft.

Jingler Mine Headstocks, Wakebridge, Crich

Built in the 1920s, these were the last surviving wooden headstocks on a Derbyshire lead mine, collapsing in 1979.

Calver Sough Mine Engine House, Calver Sough

This gritstone engine house (dated from 1858) housed a 70in (178cm) diameter cylinder Cornish pumping engine, originally built at the Bowling Iron Works at Bradford. It was partly demolished in 1929, having cost £1038.00 to construct. The 150ft (45.5m) deep shaft is covered over. In the mid-distance is the Inn at Calver Sough cross roads. The site is now occupied with bungalows.

Mandale Mine, Over Haddon

It is hard to imagine industry in Lathkilldale, but this is the remains of Mandale Mining Co's engine house built to pump water out of their lead mine. Built in 1847, it housed a steam engine built at the Milton Iron works, near Barnsley. Mining finished in 1851 and the building was partly demolished in 1852 as the engine was removed.

Copper & Tin-plate works, Oakamoor

In the 17th century a slitting mill, cutting iron sheets into thin lengths for drawing into wire, operated here. By 1761, the buildings were being used for tin-plating, which survived until at least 1807. The works continued in the copper trade until the 1960s, when operations moved to Froghall. The copper core of the first successful transatlantic cable was made here and virtually all the tram wire erected in this country was also made here, when operated by Thomas Bolton & Sons. The site is now a country park.

Below: view from the mill pond towards the road bridge works.

The south end of the works and Mill Lane.

Hartington Creamery

This factory, according to Helen Harris, (1971) commenced cheese production in the early 1870s but ceased in 1894. In 1900 J M Nuttall, a Leicestershire Stilton cheese-maker who had moved to Clifton, near Ashbourne, reopened the factory to produce Stilton once more. Rebuilt after a fire in 1929, these buildings produced Stilton until the mid-1970s when they were demolished and replaced by a modern plant. Today the manufacture of Stilton in Derbyshire is confined to this site.

Opposite Top and Bottom: Ecton Creamery

This was opened by Wilts. United Daries in 1918 and closed in 1933. It operated from former mine buildings, with the Clock House Smelter situated behind the lorry. It was served by the light railway and the latter closed in 1934.

Carsington Windmill

The tower of a former windmill survives high on the ridge above Carsington on Carsington Pasture. The top, which would house the wind-shaft and the axle to which the sails were housed, has gone. The former doorway may be seen.

The Malt House, Union Street, Ashbourne

The roasting of barley in kilns to produce malt for beer production was common. Many corn mills also produced malt as a sideline. Packhorses were used to distribute the barley and malt before roads were built to take the traditional one ton cart, ten packhorses carrying the same weight (but faster). There are references to 'great drifts' of malt-horses crossing the Peak and Derby alone had 76 malt houses. Ashbourne certainly had several and when the one in Belle Vue Road (top) was demolished, this underground store (bottom) was found.

Nestlé Milk Factory, Ashbourne

This large milk processing plant was built in 1910. It was the last in the region to take milk churns, with some coming daily from Shropshire. Now closed and demolished in 2006, it still produces raw Ashbourne water, which is treated and bottled in Leicestershire. The original chimney had a ring of white crosses at the top, set against the red of the bricks – the national flag of Switzerland.

Two views of the initial mill

Showing the view from the south (top) and the northern end (below). Milk was clearly being delivered before site works were complete (note the horse and cart by the churns).

Ashbourne Gasworks and Cattle Market

This gasworks survived long enough to see town gas being replaced by natural gas from the North Sea. The iron framing housed the gasmeter where town gas was stored. It was in Mayfield Road. The third building (adjacent to the petrol station) survives.

Part of the cattle market at Ashbourne. Taken after the removal of the cast iron pens, made in the town by W. Barnes and Co. The photo was taken in 2002 following closure of the market.

Mandale Aqueduct, Lathkilldale

Water for a waterwheel at Mandale Mine came from the lake at Carter's Mill (see p43). It crossed the valley on an aqueduct, built in 1840 and was in use for 11 years only. Remains of the piers survive (see below).

Alport Smelter, Alport, Youlgreave

In 1830, John Barker moved his lead smelter operation from Baslow to Alport. He received £250.00 (a substantial sum) towards the cost from the Duke of Devonshire, which may suggest that the latter was behind the closure. It worked lead ore and slag (the latter needing much higher temperatures). Extensive flues were built to cope with the fumes and many of these survive, although the works was demolished. It closed in 1876.

Ribden Copper Mine, Cauldon Lowe

Like the Calver Sough engine house, this one was representative of many erected across the Peak. The engine housed here had previously been at High Rake near Gt. Longstone and at Mixon Mine, south west of Ecton. It was erected here on Ingleby's shaft in 1860 on a short lived venture. The engine house was later demolished and the stone used for a limekiln at nearby Rue Hill. It apparently blew up when first fired!

Hoffman Limekiln, Harpur Hill, Buxton

This kiln was built in 1872 and operated until 1944. The chimney was demolished in 1951. The plant was operated by Buxton Lime Firms Co., later ICI, after the amalgamation of several local lime firms, including the Old Buxton Lime Kiln Co., who built this kiln.

Alsop Moor Hoffman Limekiln

Situated opposite the turn for Biggin/Hartington at the foot of Alsop Moor on the A515 was a former ICI Quarry with a Hoffman limekiln and usual tall chimney. All was removed in 1959 when quarrying ceased. Kilns had been erected here in c.1870 for brick making by Hall & Boardman. (Harris, H., 1971).

Archford Moor Limekiln, north of Alstonfield

This small and perhaps comparatively insignificant limekiln was representative of many kilns erected by farmers. It was destroyed in the 1970s. Kilns like this were part of the story of how poor Peak District soils were improved; how heath land was turned – in the 1780-1800 period – into the green fields we take for granted. Its loss destroyed a link with that time, when the way of life was changing quite significantly. We need to occasionally look back at what our forebears achieved and give more credence to their contribution to the evolution of our landscape with small lime kilns like this one.

Page Overleaf Above & Below:

Botham's Brick Works, Caldon Canal, Froghall Wharf

This is the only known photograph of Botham's Brick Works, beside the Caldon Canal at Froghall Wharf, accessed from the Foxt road. The other photograph shows the author's great uncle, Ben Porter, who was working on the construction of a brick kiln in the Manchester area. It shows well how the kilns were constructed. The photograph dates from c.1930, but the Botham's picture is older. There is no adjacent quarry, but much clay was obtained near Cauldon Lowe, this may have been where Botham's obtained their clay.

Mill Lane, Oakamoor

Looking towards the then railway and the Admiral Jervis Inn, built as a coffee house.

Page Overleaf Top:

Engine House, Milldam Mine, Great Hucklow

This photograph shows the engine house, chimney and winding gear at Milldam Mine, Great Hucklow. It was taken c.1880-1890. The Cornish-type beam can just be made out, projecting from the building and 'sitting' on the external wall. The interior end of the beam was pushed up and pulled down by the piston rod of the engine. It probably dated from c.1870, when tenders for the erection of the buildings were invited. The mine closed in 1884 and the buildings no longer survive. The shaft was 75 fathoms (450ft/136m) deep.

Hindlow Quarry, Buxton

Photographed from the A515 circa thirty years ago, neighbouring Dow Low Quarry has hardly changed. Not so the adjacent Hindlow Quarry, (seen here) which runs down to Brierlow Bar and fronts the road to Earl Sterndale and Glutton. Much of the plant shown here has been replaced by more modern equipment, no doubt producing cleaner emissions too.

Bakewell Church

By the 1820s, the fabric of the part of the building now below the spire had become unstable. As a result, the spire was taken down in 1825. The tower was taken down in 1829-30, largely at the cost of the Duke of Devonshire and the church fortunately drawn prior to the rebuilding of the crossing tower, so that it could take the weight of a new spire. This work took 11 years, from 1841-52. A large number of medieval carvings were found in the stonework during the dismantling of the rump of the crossing tower. Today they are the largest collection of such carvings in the UK. Most of them are in the porch and against the west wall of the church. This painting, in the Devonshire Collection, Chatsworth shows the church in the mid-1830s, prior to the rebuilding project.

Edensor Church

Following the rebuilding of the village of Edensor, the church was replaced. It had a west tower, with four bells. One of these survives at The Stables, Chatsworth. The new church was built in 1867 with its distinctive spire. Here are two views of the predecessor. (Naylor,D., 2005)

Ecton Chapel

This was a building built and used by Lovatt & Co., the builders of the Manifold Light Railway. In 1904, the railway was finished and the building became disused. It was purchased by Sir Thomas Wardle, of nearby Swainsley Hall, converted into a chapel and an organ provided. Sir Thomas died in January 1909 and the chapel became disused thereafter. It was later used for agricultural purposes at Wetton.

Croxden Abbey

The largest remains of a medieval abbey in the area of the Peak is at Croxden, south west of Alton, where the remains of Alton Castle – home of the abbey's benefactor – can also still be seen. Much of the abbey has been lost, but the remains are extensive, none-the-less. The majority of the buildings date from the 12th and 13th century.

Wirksworth Church

A comparison of the church as it existed between 1855 0 70 and now. The current building restored the church to much of its pre 1855 appearance, or at least that of post 1820. In 1870 the east window, which had survived the 1855 changes was replaced.

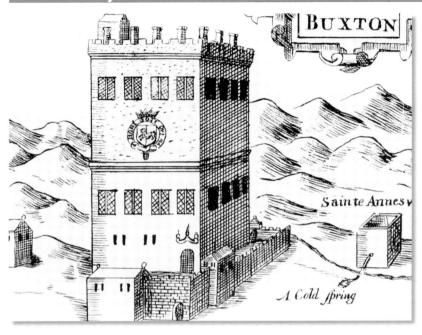

Buxton Hall, Buxton

In 1610, John Speed produced a map of Derbyshire. It included a drawing of the original Buxton Hall. This four-storey building was thought to have been lost, but some good detective work brought the realisation that it still survived within the fabric of the current building. It now faces St Annes Well and is the section with the two three-storey bays. The fourth floor is mostly below pavement level. This is the building in which Mary, Queen of Scots stayed.

The Haddon Hall Hydro, London Road, Buxton

This hydro opened in 1903 with 50 bedrooms. It was a late-comer to the hydropathic business in Buxton, the first being the Malvern House Hydro, which opened in 1866. The Haddon Hall Hydro later became offices and is now empty, boarded up and with its future very much at risk.

The Buxton Hydro, Hartington Street, Buxton

The Malvern House Hydro originally built in 1866 by the Revd. James Shaw. He previously had run the Matlock House Hydro in Matlock, opening with a capacity for 40 patients. Mike Langham records that in 1884 it could take 180 patients. A further large extension, the building nearest the camera, pushed this up to 260 rooms in 1899, when it became the Buxton Hydro. The site is now occupied by a housing development.

The Empire Hotel, Buxton

The Empire opened in 1903 and was the most luxurious hotel in Buxton. It had capacity for 300 guests and was built by Spiers & Pond, who ran high-class restaurant cars on the railways. It was requisitioned by the Army during the Great War and never reopened as a hotel. Lying empty for a long time, it was demolished in 1964. It was situated to the rear of the Palace Hotel, in close proximity to the railway. See also p.140

The Ball Inn, Middleton Dale

The Ball Inn, formerly at the junction of Eyam and Middleton Dales. Taken in 1919, an earlier view shows that the nearest building had been a barn and the right hand building was relatively new. All have now been demolished.

Cat & Fiddle Inn, west of the Upper Goyt Valley

Of course this popular inn still exists. Here is a view of it when first built.

Wheatsheaf Hotel, Ashbourne

This Georgian building actually survives, although much altered. Situated at the end of Dig Street, it was a coaching inn. In 1820, its landlord made his own beer, known as 'Tear Brain'! Here is a view of the building prior to alteration. The front has changed significantly and the archway lost.

St John's Street, Ashbourne

Ashbourne still has at least two timber-framed buildings, but another survived until the first half of the 20th century. It stood adjacent to the former Wheatsheaf Hotel and was probably at least 400 years old. Bookthrift now occupy the site. Another view is used overleaf. Note the barber's pole.

The Pavilion, Matlock Bath
This massive structure was on the site of Gulliver's Kingdom, above the Royal Hotel.

Many of our railway lines and stations succumbed to the Beeching axe. Here are a few, hopefully representative scenes, recalling the days when we had both through and branch-line services. Today we have services to Matlock and Buxton, plus the through route from Manchester to Sheffield via Edale. Talk of rebuilding the line between Buxton and Matlock looks as far away as ever, although Peak Rail use the rails to Rowsley.

Chinley Station
This is the former station.

Millers Dale Station

This served the Midland Railway's Derby-Manchester line and the branch to Buxton.

Bakewell Station

Now an industrial estate occupies the site of the station.

Rowsley Station

The passenger station, which closed in 1967.

This goods yard existed at Rowsley on the site of the outlet village. This was the original station of 1849.

A lovely scene of Rowsley goods yard, taken pre-1923 in Midland Railway days.

Matlock Bath Station

Although still open, this scene has long since disappeared, although the main building survives.

Sheep Pasture Incline on the Cromford & High Peak Railway

Rolling stock was hauled up by a surviving steam engine, situated above the village of Middleton-by-Wirksworth and easily found because of its high chimney.

Middleton Incline

Ron Duggins captured the final days of this line. The building (left) survives as a ruin.

Longdendale

Post-Beeching this offered, for a while, an alternative to the Hope Valley line before it was closed and the track lifted.

These two views were taken near to Crowden.

Matlock Station

Like Buxton it still provides rail services, but prospects for the reconstruction of the rail link between the two towns seem as far away as ever. Maybe the carbon footprint opportunity cost (of more and more visitor's cars) will eventually be offset against the spiralling capital cost of reinstatement.

The station in 1986. One of several views from Ron Duggin's *Echoes of the Dales: The 1960s*

Ashbourne Station
The pre-1890 N.S.R., station, removed for the station shown below.

The station in 1956. It closed 1st June 1964.

Seven Arches Bridge, Ashbourne

Just north of Ashbourne tunnel was Seven Arches Bridge. It was a brick-built structure carrying the railway over the Sow Brook. It collapsed under what many local people believed to be suspicious circumstances when the Tissington Trail was being laid down, in April 1980.

Tissington Station

Hindlow Station

Situated close to Hindlow lime works. The rails are still there (single line now), but the buildings were removed in 1967.

Parsley Hay Station

The platforms and most buildings here were removed in 1965, prior to the creation of the railway trails.

Buxton Station

The two stations at Buxton with the demolished Midland station nearest the camera. It fell under the axe of Dr. Beeching.

Waterhouses Station

Here the narrow gauge Manifold line met the branch line from Leek. The Manifold closed in 1934 after just 30 years. The Manifold Valley stations were wooden, prefabricated buildings made in Fleetwood. They survived the closure of the line, but were demolished following a spate of vandalism. Bottom: Wetton Mill Station.

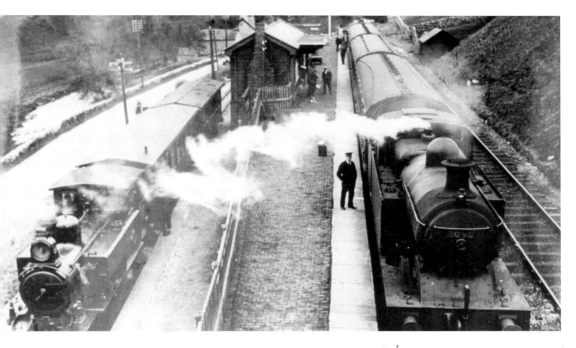

Hulme End Station

Only the goods shed survives at Waterhouses, but the waiting room is now a Visitor Centre at Hulme End. The carriage shed (on the right) was demolished years ago, but the engine shed survived. Refurbished in 2006, only two of the supporting stanchions were re-useable. The rest of the building is new. Site works remain incomplete and the building unused with no budget to finish it; what a farce. The water tower has also gone.

Leek Station

This differed from the line's rural buildings. These horses, with their traps, contend with a blizzard as they await the next train. The site is now a supermarket car park.

The Churnet Valley

The Churnet Valley had several tramways, feeding coal, limestone and iron ore down to the canal. This bridge carried the iron ore (from Kingsley Far Banks and the mines of W. Bowers) over the River Churnet to a wharf near what is now known as Podmore's lock.

Two early tramways

Built to convey limestone were the Caldon, dating from 1778, which ran from Cauldon Lowe (sic) to Froghall and the Caldon Canal. It was the first line to be built under a legislative enactment. Four lines were built here in all, closing finally in 1920. This view was near the top of the line.

The Peak Forest Tramway

This connected Bugsworth Basin (later Buxsworth) on the Peak Forest Canal with the limestone quarries in the Dove Holes area, north of Buxton. It was in use in 1799. Twenty years later, the Canal Company started extracting limestone on the Duke of Devonshire's Peak Forest estate. In the first 12 years, no less than 601,740 tons was extracted, with presumably most, if not all, going down to the canal. This was probably the start of Peak Dale Quarry. This scene shows the line heading for Chapel-en-le-Frith. It became completely disused by 1926.

Uttoxeter Canal

The Caldon Canal formerly continued on from Froghall to Uttoxeter. This branch closed in January 1847. A bridge (Seventy Bridge) and lock (California Lock) survive together with various lengths of canal. Here is the lock, between Froghall and Oakamoor (and off the right of way). All woodwork has long disappeared, but the masonry seems reasonably sound.

The reverse view and site of the upper lock gate.

Buxworth Basin, Whaley Bridge

This is the site of the former wharf building. It spanned the canal and gave undercover facilities for the tran shipment of goods – particularly important in the case of lime. Holes for the roof tie beams spanning the cana can be seen.

Leek Wharf

In this instance, the whole wharf has gone – at Leek, on a branch of the Caldon. It was situated on the wes side of the railway station and the line maybe seen in the background.

Matlock Bridge

This was in existence in the mid-thirteenth century. When it was widened early in the last century, the original packhorse-bridge was found within the structure and still in good condition. This scene shows the upstream side of the bridge in 1802. The current bridge retains four pointed arches on the downsteam side.

Hanging Bridge, Mayfield, Ashbourne

Fortunately the medieval bridge (seen here) on the current A52 was retained when widened in 1937. 'Hanging' refers to the steeply sloping land on the west side of the bridge. Don't be confused by the nearby Gallows Tree Lane!

Longnor

Mention has been made above to the loss of property in the Via Gellia owing to road widening (see p 118). Many properties have been lost or truncated in this way. The widening of Monyash Road at Bakewell and the loss of part of the preserved corn mill at Leek, come to mind. Here is another example of buildings removed at Longnor opposite to the Cheshire Cheese Inn.

Brund Bridge, Sheen

Many bridges have been widened or rebuilt. Here is a view of Brund Mill Bridge, over the River Manifold, which was rebuilt in 1891.

Errwood, Goyt Valley

Two bridges existed at Goyts Bridge. The packhorse bridge (seen below and overleaf top) was rebuilt higher up the valley beyond the Errwood Reservoir in the 1960s. The other is still in situ and visible under conditions of drought.

Cock Bridge, Ashopton

This bridge crossed the River Ashop at its confluence with the River Derwent. It is now under Ladybower Reservoir.

Edensor School

Built as a boy's school in 1841, the original school was replaced by this building, which survived until 1950. Dianne Naylor (2005) states that the design is attributed to Robertson and was typical of several village schools portrayed in Loudon's Encyclopedia of 'pure Italian' style.

Bakewell Cinema

Bakewell Picture House, Matlock Street.

Matlock Cinema

Situated on Steep Turnpike and Causeway Lane. It was originally The Cinema House, later the Ritz. It is now in several occupations.

Buxton Cinema, Spring Gardens

Taken in 1985

Empire Cinema, Ashbourne

This is the Empire Cinema built behind the Station Hotel (now The Beresford Hotel) by Eades, brewers of Burton-on-Trent, who also built the hotel. It had seating for 650 and opened on Whit Monday, 27th May 1912. However, the electricity failed and the first films were shown a week later. It was Ashbourne's first cinema and leased to Edgar Stebbing. The building has been rebuilt and is still called The Empire, but is no longer a cinema.

The next group of photographs portray a group of buildings, some of them gone, that have changed use. They were all youth hostels, helping to bring in a phenomena which brought the countryside to thousands who had never been there. The surge of youth hostel openings in 1930 passed by the Peak, the first one being Errwood Hall Farm in 1931 (closing in 1935). Ilam opened in 1932 but only as a small operation, which may have been open when the current building opened in 1935, thereby being the oldest to survive. See also Derwent Hall (p.9)

Shining Cliff Youth Hostel, Alderwasley

This youth hostel opened in 1947 in a building provided by The Griff Pioneers. It was initially of timber construction, similar to many early youth hostels, when the amount of money available to provide and furnish the building was hard to come by. This one was destroyed by fire in the 1970s, which turned out to be a blessing, for the current building is a significant improvement. It is situated in the woods above Ambergate, formerly part of the Hurt estate at Alderwasley Hall, but was closed in 2007, when the lease ended.

Dimmingsdale Youth Hostel, Oakamoor

This youth hostel opened in 1941, being run by Mrs Weston, who sold it to the YHA in 1950. The hostel was a collection of wooden huts, with one of them portrayed here. A large wooden chicken hut divided down its length served both sexes. Another hut was situated close to a cliff edge and was a second womens' dormitory.

The common-room-cum-member's-kitchen was in a clearing in the wood, probably where the current youth hostel stands. Icy cold water was available in the wash huts that were 'quite a distance' away. (unpublished MS by M. Burton). All quite in keeping with the spartan conditions of the early 1930s when the young movement was getting started.

Dovedale Tea Room

This was one of at least three North Staffordshire tea-rooms – Thor's Cave, Beeston Tor and Dovedale. The first two were adjacent to the Manifold Valley Light Railway and the third (shown here) was at Ilam Rock. Tearooms were a common place a hundred years ago, although the use of these three places must have been very seasonal. The Beeston Tor building still survives, an unusual survivor of early recreational activity in pre-Planning Act days. In late 1906, an opportunist thief broke into all three of these buildings on the same night.

Left: Thor's Cave; below: Ilam Rock; bottom: Beeston Tor

Rudyard Lake Tea Room

The wooded west bank of Rudyard Lake had many temporary 'holiday cottages' finished with corrugated iron on a wooden frame. The reservoir was a popular recreational area. This advert for Mrs Heath's tearoom recalls this temporary village. Spite Hall House was built directly in front of another large villa to block its view of the lake.

Mrs. HEATH,

Spite Hall, Rudyard Vale.

Ashbourne Open-air Swimming Pool

This pool has also gone, but probably with no regrets from its former users. Many school children, forced into its ice-covered water in early springtime, have good reason to remember it! It was situated on Belle Vue Road, overlooking St. Oswald's Church. The site has been redeveloped with housing.

Little Hayfield Open-air Swimming Pool

This open-air pool with its statues and terraces was certainly unusual, but regrettably it no longer survives.

Shooting Cabin, Kinder Scout

This shooting cabin was photographed in 1902 in Grindsbrook Clough. Two maids stand in the doorway. A group of visitors sit in front of the small marquee. This was in the days before general access onto Kinder Scout was permitted. The cabin no longer exists.

Opposite Above & Below:

Clifton & Sturston Mills, nr Ashbourne

These two water-powered corn mills either side of Ashbourne used to be the goals in the town's annual Shrovetide football game. Ashbourne is the last town in England to play hug football at Shrovetide. The waterwheels became the goals when the game switched to being played along the valley bottom in c.1798. Previously, the goals were north and south of the River Henmore, the goals changing frequently. Clifton Mill was demolished in 1967 and Sturston Mill a few years later. A plinth on the riverbank is now the goal. The game is as much a part of our heritage as any building – it portrays human recreational social behaviour of 500 years ago. The Derby hug football game at Shrovetide lasted until 1846 and gave soccer the term 'a Derby game' when two local teams play each other. Access is possible at the Clifton site only.

The Pump Room, Buxton

Buxton must have had a craze on cupolas and still has quite a few, although these two on the Pump Room opposite The Crescent no longer grace the buildings. It was once a popular place to take the water. Although the facilities remain at St. Annes Well, the Pump Room is unused. The collonade has also gone.

Inside the Pump Room (in the 1930s?), visitors take the water.

Paradise Walk, Ilam

This small suspension bridge spanning the River Manifold at Paradise Walk, Ilam. It was lost when a tree fell across it in the severe storm of 1962. Another one crossed Fernilee Reservoir, but was removed when Errwood Reservoir was built, with a road across the dam.

'The Spa of Blue Waters', Buxton

Buxton water may be known across the land, but the Spa era has now gone. These are the Hot Baths, but not those originally built in 1854 by Henry Currey.

The Pavilion, Buxton

Although still standing, this building has seen significant minor alterations.

The wrecker's ball at work on the Empire Hotel, Buxton, 1964

OTHER LOCAL TITLES AVAILABLE FROM LANDMARK PUBLISHING

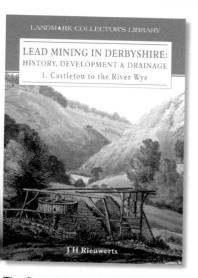

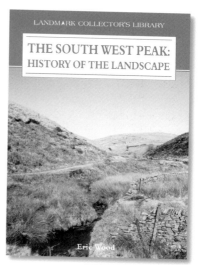

The first of three Limited Edition volumes.
192pp, 246x174mm, HB, with 16pp colour and numerous mono illustrations, £25.00

This book shows many examples of how the Moorlands have changed over the years.
96pp, 246x174mm, PB, £9.99

Covers the landscape history of the area between Buxton, Leek & Macclesfield.
192pp, 246x174mm, PB, £19.99

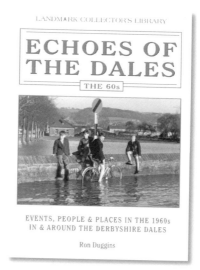

96pp, 246x174mm, PB, with over 200 mono illustrations of the Derbyshire Dales in the 1950s, £9.99

96pp, 246x174mm, PB, the latest in a series of books on the Derbyshire Dales in the 1960s, £9.99

LOOK OUT FOR ECHOES OF THE DALES: THE 1970s

MEMORIES OF ANDREW DEVONSHIRE

Deborah Devonshire

The life of the 11th Duke in photographs. 112pp, 246mmx174mm, PB, £9.99

A collection of photographs recalling the life of the longest serving Duke of Devonshire. Many aspects of his life are portrayed in this compelling and most readable of books. The majority of photographs have been taken from the family albums of the author, Deborah Devonshire.